MORE
BRAAI
★ THE ★
BELOVED
COUNTRY

JEAN NEL

ACKNOWLEDGEMENTS

My mother, Salome Nel, represented all that is good in this world. She was a constant source of encouragement and the hardest-working, most dedicated person I have ever known. Ma, thank you for the 'love of food' genes you passed on to me.

Thank you Keith Barclay for your persistence so many years ago. Without you I wouldn't have been around the fire.

Myburgh du Plessis, a mighty talented photographer, thank you for the magnificent photographs and finding the *pièce de résistance* in every image.

To my publisher, Bridget Impey, thank you! To the amazing Jacana Media team that helped get this project to the finishing line: Nadia Goetham for making sure that deadlines were met with the production, Lara Jacob and Meg Mance for their days of work on my recipes and copy, Shawn Paikin for designing this beautiful book and Janine Daniel for getting the marketing on board.

Russel Wasserfall, for guiding me into the world of publishing. I'll never forget it.

My Greek friend, Linda Papapetros, thank you for your friendship spanning over many years. Thank you for your advice and wisdom, and for the most stunning props used for this book.

My two assistants, Lindelwa Ndunge and Zandile Gqobho, thank you for pushing the boundaries during the production of this book. I adore you both.

To the best team in the world — Amy Whittam, Niell Grobler, Maurizio Grossi, Christo Vermeulen and Tommy Dickson — thank you for the Weber braais, but most of all for believing in me.

Mari-Lise Naude Rabie, thank you for your and Andrew Rabie hospitality while shooting this book. Klein Dasvlei captured my heart.

Providores of excellence, who has helped set the standard in the South African food industry, you are an essential part of my working life. Andries and Louise Rabie, thank you for the best olive oil in the world. Kathleen Quililnan, thank you for the best pestos and other exotics.

Fiona Mckie, you are my greatest critic but I guess one of my biggest fans too. Thank you for your encouragement.

Oliver Pywell and Jill Barrington-Roberts, thank you for finding the best blue shirts that I was adamant I wanted to wear while braaiing.

Shireen Oliver-Lakey, your attention to detail for finding the right colour plates ... pure perfection.

Raymond and Janine van Niekerk, thank you for your ongoing support through the years. Life would be simply boring without you!

Abigail Donnelly, thank you for your advice, recipe ideas and your friendship.

Jakes Potgieter, who will be with us friends around a fire real soon. We love you.

BRAAI – AN INTRODUCTION ix

IN THE FIRE 1
    Sticky Chicken Wings 2
    Prawns and Chorizo 4
    Braaied Whole Squid with Chilli and Mint 6
    Mealies with Mayo, Feta & Lime 8
    Mussels with Lemon & Curry Butter 10
    Braaied Asparagus with Sesame Salt 12
    Korean Beef Ribs 14
    Bacon Jam on Braaied Rosemary Flatbreads 16
    Crumbed Brown Mushrooms on the Braai 18
    Tuna Steak with Romesco Sauce & Braaied Leeks 20
    Boerewors in an East-West Sauce 22
    Haloumi with Pomegranate-Mint Salsa 24

DIRECT COOKING 27
    T-bone Florentine 28
    Pork Chops with Strawberry and Balsamic Vinegar Sauce 30
    Greek Fish Sosaties with Tzaziki 32
    Prawn Peri-peri Skewers 34
    Chicken Breasts with Aromatic Indian Spices 36
    Chicken Pesto Sandwich 38
    Brazilian Rump Kebabs with Smoky Tomato-Pepper Salsa .. 40

Coffee-rubbed Rib-eye Steak with a Buttermilk-Gorgonzola Cheese Sauce 42

Mexican Chicken Wrap Party 44

Lamb Burger with Guacamole 46

My Spicy Lamb Chops 48

Latin Mojo Pork Fillet 50

Boerewors Coil with Tomato Smoor 52

Greek Lamb Sosaties with Caper-Mint Salsa 54

Eastern Ostrich Fillet 56

Thai Green Chicken Curry in a Wok 58

Game Sosaties in a Buttermilk, Red Wine & Honey Marinade 60

South African Curried Apricot Chicken Kebabs 62

Sirloin Steak with Tabasco Butter 64

INDIRECT COOKING 67

Braaied Beef Fillet with Chimmichurri 68

Sticky Asian Pork Neck 70

Pork Belly with a Quince and Old Brown Sherry Sauce 72

Beer Can Chicken 74

Spatchcock Chicken 76

Harissa Chicken 78

Chilli Caramel Chicken Thighs 80

Thai Norwegian Salmon in Foil 82

Garlic and Rosemary Lamb Loin 84

Chermoula Butter Fish 86

Brandy & Coke Pork Ribs 88

Lebanese Leg of Lamb with Pomegranate Salad 90

SIDES FROM THE FIRE 93

BLT Salad 94

Pan Potatoes in the Fire 96

Korean Mushrooms with Soy, Sesame & Ginger 98

Melted Brie on a Plank 100

Potato Wedges with Homemade Tomato Relish	102
Chilli Salt Pineapple Skewers	104
Sweet Potato Salad	106
Garlic & Parmesan Bread	108
Roosterkoek with Rooibos & Bacon	110
Braaibroodjies	112

SIDES FROM THE KITCHEN ... 115

Grilled Red Onion Salad with Feta & Almond-Chilli Salsa	116
Chakalaka Bread	118
Roasted Spiced Cauliflower Salad with Grapes	120
Watermelon Salad	122
Beans & Olive Salad with Balsamic Onions	124
Cabbage Salad	126
Caprese Salad	128
Guacamole	130
Pickled Cucumbers	132
Pea & Parmesan Risotto	134
Biltong Salad	136
Braai Sauce	138
The All Season Rub	138
Olive Oil-baked Potatoes	140
Quinoa Salad	142
Nuts for the Braai	144
Old-fashioned Potato Salad	146
Beetroot, Walnut & Feta Salad	148

INDEX ... 150

Wherever specified, salt means flaked sea salt and pepper means freshly ground black pepper. Oil refers to the olive oil you prefer to use unless cooking oil is specified and this refers to household vegetable oil. All recipes serve 4 to 6 people.

BRAAI
AN INTRODUCTION

Klein Dasvlei

A great braai stays with you, as does the experience of braaiing. Some of my happiest memories have been around the fire. I am on a quest to share my passion for the braai as it was ignited in me so many years ago. But I somehow have a strong feeling that you also have some great memories around the fire and your braai.

In *Braai the Beloved Country* I wrote about how the braai in my being is a strong fire. The flames have been burning stronger the past few years as we braaied continuously at events, weddings and everyday catering. A kettle braai is never far away from me. I even have braai wood in my catering vehicles as one never knows when and where an opportunity will arise.

Fires lure people to gather around, and yes they do stay awhile. Braaiing is relaxing and will occupy you for a good few hours. I do hope the recipes inside this book ignite the fire and adventure in you too. Go to your *agterplaas*, your backyard, and light the fire!

I have picked different cuts of meat for the recipes in this book. I can assure you they are all the very best. Alternative types of meat will encourage you to think outside your normal braai routine. Forget about lamb chops and a piece of wors for once. Push the boundaries around the fire. I am also sure it will save you a little bit of money, as certain cuts of meat are more affordable than others. These recipes are the ones that I use in my boutique catering company. If you want to smoke some meat, the Mexican Chicken Wrap and the Lamb Loin is so well suited for that type of cooking.

A good braai is not only about meat. I don't expect you to live off the braai (though that won't be a tragic fate). Please explore the recipes from In the Flames, Sides from the Fire and Sides from the Kitchen in this book and your dinner table will be laden with the best braaied meats, salads, vegetables and breads.

I like to share my braai secrets and you're all invited to spend an afternoon with me at my Braai Academy in Cape Town.

So light the fire and let's braai.

BRAAI METHODS

DIRECT HEAT

For this method, the food is placed directly over the fire of a charcoal braai or open fire. (All Direct recipes in this book are suited either for your kettle braai or for the open fire using wood, except for the Thai Green Chicken, which is only suited for the kettle braai.) The food cooks relatively quickly, usually in less than 25 minutes over very intense heat, which sears and caramelises the surface. If you plan to use any basting sauce with sugar on the meat, do it just before it comes off the braai. Sauces with sugar can burn easily when exposed to the intense heat of a direct heat braai.

Cuts to use: burgers, steaks, chops, pork fillet, boneless chicken pieces, kebabs, fish fillets, prawns and vegetables

INDIRECT HEAT

For this method the food is placed away from the heat source, so it cooks from reflected heat. Separate the charcoal into two mounds on opposite sides of the kettle braai or use two charcoal bins with briquettes for this method.

Cuts to use: whole chickens, leg of lamb, pork neck, ribs, any bone-in chicken pieces

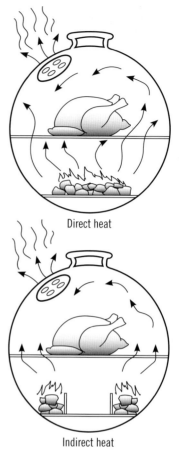

Direct heat

Indirect heat

PUT A LID ON IT

This is the one of the main questions we discuss and debate in a braai class or corporate event. I find that for most home braaiers, to have the lid on is the answer. Covering the kettle braai creates convection-like heat, which helps to braai the food evenly and more quickly. It is critical to cover the kettle braai when you use the Indirect method. I personally use the Direct method, followed by the Indirect method in some of the recipes in this book, the Beef Fillet Chimmichurri being just one of them.

LET'S SEASON THE MEAT

Rubs and marinades are tasty ways to add flavour to meat before and after it's braaied. However, if you braai with high-quality meat all you need is a hot fire and some salt and pepper for the flavour to shine through.

It is crucial to salt the meat before and after it's braaied. For thick cuts of steak, lamb or pork, season 20 minutes before the braai and let the meat rest on a wire rack. For thinner fillets, cutlets, fish fillets and vegetables, season just before you braai. When seasoning, sprinkle salt all over the piece of meat, especially the edges and the ends.

After braaiing, slice the meat and top with salt.

A few cranks of a peppermill can do wonders to anything on the braai. However, using coarsely ground black pepper is better for bigger cuts of meats.

IS THE MEAT DONE YET?

Meat will continue to cook even after you remove it from the braai. Please take this into consideration. Different pieces of meat will not hit their perfect doneness at the exact same moment, even if you place them on the braai at the same time. Each meat varies from piece to piece, as does the fire temperature beneath them.

The ability to know when the meat is done is probably the most important skill of any braaier. When you braai meat becomes firmer to the touch. Chefs can judge the degree of doneness of a piece of meat by pushing it with a finger and assessing its doneness. I call this the Hand method. Practice it and over time you will become an expert. Or use a thermometer to help with the guesswork. I must confess that I have never used one though.

CLEANING AND SEASONING THE BRAAI

Brushing and oiling the braai grid is an integral part of the process. Most of the time when food sticks to the braai grid, it is because the braai was not hot enough nor clean enough in the first place. So prepare your braai by cleaning and oiling it.

The best way to clean a braai is with heat and so the perfect time to clean it is directly after you have used it. Use a good quality wire brush and some elbow force to clean the braai grids. An oiled kitchen towel can be used to rub the braai surface. It's called pure braai hygiene.

LIGHTING THE COALS

Place lightly crushed newspaper sheets (2 or 3 sheets maximum) on the bottom of a chimney starter. Don't use too much or you'll smother the fire. Fill the chimney with briquettes then light the paper. The fire will burn upward and ignite the fuel. In 15 to 20 minutes the coals should be covered in grey ash and glowing ready for the braai.

CONTROLLING THE HEAT

As I said in *Braai the Beloved Country* – test a fire by holding your hand 2 centimetres over the braai grid. You should be able to hold your hand there for two seconds if you want a hot fire, and 4 seconds for a medium. Adjust the vents of your kettle braai to adjust the temperature – open for more heat and close for less heat.

DEALING WITH FLARE-UPS

Any braaier will experience a flare-up once a while. It is inevitable. Honestly, they are not that terrible, so do not run off when you experience it. Most flare-ups die quickly. Simply move the meat to the colder side of the braai and wait for the flames to die. Forget about throwing water on the fire. Ash will be all over your food.

BRAAI DO'S AND DON'TS

DO'S

- Understand the difference between Direct and Indirect method braaiing.
- Keep the braai grates clean; otherwise your food will taste stale.
- Oil the braai grates to prevent the food from sticking.
- Leave the food directly over a hot fire just enough to caramelise, but never so long that it blackens.
- Turn meat only once while braaiing, if possible, unless specified. It will cook more evenly.
- Let the meat rest after you take it off the braai. The meat juices need to redistribute, ensuring juiciness and better flavour.
- Read and follow the maintenance schedule of your a new kettle braai.

DON'TS

- Never rush when braaiing. What's the need to rush?
- Cheap food will taste cheap, so purchase good-quality ingredients.
- Always have a few bags of wood or charcoal on stand-by.
- Purchase charcoal from only a known-name company.
- Make sure your food is at room temperature to ensure even braaiing.
- Don't put a hot chimney starter on or near anything that's flammable.

My advice for the perfect braai chicken wings, plain and simple: go low. A medium-to-low heat is what is required with 20 minutes or a bit more for perfect wings.

INGREDIENTS

16 chicken wings

STICKY SAUCE

125ml lemon juice
125ml soya sauce
90ml tomato sauce
70g smooth apricot jam
4 garlic cloves, chopped finely

Mix all the ingredients for the sticky sauce. Set aside.

Marinate the chicken wings with 90ml of the sticky sauce.

Place the chicken wings on a clean, hinged grid or use some skewers for easy handling and even braaiing.

Place the grid on a medium-to-low fire. Braai the chicken wings for between 20 and 30 minutes, turning frequently. Baste with the rest of the sticky sauce in the last 5 minutes of cooking time.

PRAWNS AND CHORIZO

The chorizo in this recipe makes everything taste better as does the paprika and the garlic. The lemon cuts through the richness of the prawns and chorizo. I promise you — you will lick your plate.

INGREDIENTS

150g chorizo, cut in 1cm slices

30ml olive oil

3 garlic cloves, crushed

400g medium-sized prawns, deveined and butterflied

15ml chilli flakes

Juice and zest of 2 lemons

30ml flat-leaf parsley, chopped

30ml coriander leaves, chopped

Freshly ground black pepper

Crusty bread and lemons, to serve

Heat a frying pan over a hot fire but not directly over the flames. Add the chorizo and stir fry for up to 3 minutes. Remove the pan from the fire and discard most of the oil. Set the chorizo aside. Add the olive oil to the pan. Add garlic and stir fry for a minute. Add the prawns and chilli flakes, and stir fry for a minute. Add the lemon juice and chorizo, and cook until prawns turn opaque. Sprinkle with the lemon zest, parsley and coriander, and season. Take it off the fire and serve it in the pan with crusty bread and more lemon.

BRAAIED WHOLE SQUID
WITH CHILLI AND MINT

Forget about rings for a bit and try this cut of this fabulous bounty from the sea! Ask your fishmonger to clean the squid for you if you don't want to do it yourself. Use a griddled, cast iron pan for the recipe or a pan.

INGREDIENTS

10 medium-sized squid, cleaned and prepared whole

30ml fennel seeds

Salt and freshly ground black pepper to taste

2 lemons, halved

45ml olive oil

2–3 red chillies, seeded and sliced

Handful of fresh mint, torn

Lay the squid flat on a surface and insert a large knife flat inside the ring. Slice the squid with another knife as you would slice for rings. The knife inside of the body of the squid will prevent you from cutting right through. You end up with a concertina effect but the squid will hold together.

Grind the fennel seeds together with the salt and pepper, and sprinkle over the squid. Braai the squid immediately on a hot braai, turning every 30 seconds. This should not take longer than a few minutes.

Transfer squid to a bowl. Drizzle with olive oil, lemon juice, chillies and mint.

MEALIES WITH MAYO, FETA & LIME

Indulge in this classic Mexican combination of mayonnaise, chilli and cheese the next time you braai mealies.

INGREDIENTS

4 mealies with husks
45ml mayonnaise
Pinch of cayenne pepper
200g feta, crumbled
125ml chopped coriander
Lime or lemon, cut in halves

Pull the husks back from the mealies, leaving them attached to the base, but discard the hair. Soak in cold water for 15 minutes.

Lightly oil the braai grid. Braai the mealies, turning occasionally for about 10–15 minutes. The kernels should be tender and browned. Remove mealies from the braai.

Whisk together the mayonnaise and cayenne pepper in a bowl. Brush the mayonnaise onto the hot corn, then sprinkle with the crumbled feta and chopped coriander. Serve with lemon or lime halves.

MUSSELS WITH LEMON & CURRY BUTTER

Cooking these mussels on the open fire always reminds me of the big pots of fresh mussels we eat at Isabella Nichaus's house along the West Coast. The butter can be used on just about any fish.

Add half the butter, spring onions, lemon rind, turmeric, ginger, garlic and lemon juice to a small pan and cook over a medium heat until butter has softened and become aromatic. Put in a bowl and add the remaining butter and chopped herbs. Cover and set aside.

Place a pan on a medium-to-high-heat fire. Add the mussels and wine. Cook until the mussels start to open. Discard any that don't open. Add the butter to the mussel pan to melt and take mussels off the fire.

INGREDIENTS

1kg fresh West Coast mussels, beards removed and scrubbed

60ml white wine

CURRY BUTTER

60g butter, softened

2 spring onions, finely chopped

30ml grated lemon rind

15ml turmeric

15ml finely grated fresh ginger

2 garlic cloves, crushed

30ml lemon juice

Chopped coriander, flat-leaf parsley and mint leaves

Salt and freshly ground black pepper to taste

BRAAIED ASPARAGUS WITH SESAME SALT

Toasted sesame seeds with salt is a staple in my kitchen. I use it for stir fries, sometimes even in salads.

INGREDIENTS

400g asparagus, trimmed
30ml olive oil

SESAME SALT

45ml sesame seeds
15ml salt flakes

Lightly toast the sesame seeds in a small pan over a low heat. Add salt flakes and store in a jar.

Lightly brush the asparagus with the olive oil. Braai the asparagus on medium coals or use a heated, lightly oiled griddle pan. Braai between 4–5 minutes only, depending on the size of the asparagus. Add the sesame salt to the asparagus and serve.

KOREAN BEEF RIBS

Sweet, salt, tangy, lick-it-off-your fingers ribs. It is best to marinate the ribs overnight for the best results. This marinade go very well with pork or chicken.

INGREDIENTS

8–10 beef ribs, cut 2–3 cm thick

MARINADE

125ml soy sauce
90g brown sugar
30ml rice vinegar
60ml sesame oil
4 cloves garlic, finely crushed
15ml fresh ginger, crushed
30ml tomato sauce
15ml chilli flakes

Combine the soy sauce, brown sugar, vinegar, sesame oil, garlic, ginger, tomato sauce and chilli flakes in a bowl, and whisk till the sugar dissolve. Place ribs in a large zip-lock bag and pour marinate over. Seal the bag and refrigerate overnight. Turn the zip-lock bag a few times while in the refrigerator.

Bring ribs to room temperature an hour before your braai.

Remove the ribs from the marinade and pat them dry with a kitchen towel. Place the ribs directly over the fire and braai, turning once until medium. This should take 8 to 10 minutes. Heat the sauce in a small pan on the fire. Brush the ribs with the sauce the last 2 minutes while on the braai.

BACON JAM ON BRAAIED ROSEMARY FLATBREADS

I fell in love with Neil Roakes's bacon jam recipe. It's now a staple in my kitchen.

INGREDIENTS

FOR THE BACON JAM

250g bacon, chopped in 1cm pieces
3 large white onions, finely sliced
15ml dried chilli flakes
1 red chilli, chopped
5 cloves garlic, finely chopped
15ml mustard seeds
80g brown sugar
90ml balsamic vinegar
Salt and freshly ground black pepper

FOR THE FLATBREADS

250g bread flour
30ml active dry yeast
30ml salt
30ml chopped fresh rosemary
200ml hot water
30ml olive oil plus more for brushing

Thank you, Neil Roake, for allowing me to share your bacon jam recipe (from *More Life's a Beach Cottage*).

Add the bacon to a large frying pan, over a medium heat. Fry for 5–6 minutes, remove from the pan and set aside. Keep some of the bacon fat in the pan. Add the onions and sweat until translucent. This should take between 8 and 10 minutes. Add the chilli, garlic, mustard seeds and brown sugar, and stir until the onion caramelises. Add the balsamic vinegar, stir and let it cook for another 10 minutes. It's crucial that you stay close to the jam now or it may burn. Add the bacon bits, stir through and season. The jam should be of a sticky consistency when done.

For the flatbreads, sift the flour into a large bowl. Stir in the yeast, salt and rosemary. Make a well in the centre, then add the hot water and olive oil and mix to make a soft dough. Turn out onto a lightly floured work surface. Knead until the dough is smooth and elastic.

Shape the dough into a ball, then put in an oiled bowl. Cover with a clean dish towel and let it rise in a warm place for 50–60 minutes. It should double in size.

Punch down the dough and divide into quarters. Roll each piece out on a lightly floured work surface to make a 8–10cm long oval.

Brush the bread dough with a little olive oil and braai over a low heat for 5–6 minutes. Brush the top with olive oil, turn over and braai for a further 4–5 minutes. Spread the bacon jam over the hot flatbreads and serve.

Crumbed Brown Mushrooms on the Braai

Brown mushrooms have a meaty texture. These are delicious eaten straight off the braai. Use a heated cast iron pan for these beauties and braai over a medium-to-low-heat fire.

INGREDIENTS

- 2–3 eggs
- 2 garlic cloves, finely chopped
- 30g breadcrumbs
- 60g all-purpose flour
- 30ml lemon zest, grated
- 15ml chopped thyme or rosemary
- 8–10 medium-sized brown mushrooms
- Some all-purpose flour for dusting
- 90ml olive oil
- Salt and freshly ground black pepper

Beat the eggs with the garlic in a bowl. Add seasoning. Set aside.

Combine breadcrumbs, flour, lemon zest and fresh herbs in a bowl.

Dust mushrooms lightly with flour. Dip mushrooms in the egg mixture and then in the breadcrumb mixture.

Lightly oil a heated cast iron pan. Place mushrooms in the pan and braai for 8–10 minutes.

TUNA STEAK
WITH ROMESCO SAUCE & BRAAIED LEEKS

Romesco sauce is a classic Spanish salsa that goes very well with tuna and pork. It is easy to make and can be stored for up to a week. This recipe requires the lid to be off as long as the tuna steaks are on the braai.

INGREDIENTS

4 x 200g tuna steaks
Olive oil
Salt
1 lemon
4–6 baby leeks or spring onions

FOR THE ROMESCO SAUCE

2 large red peppers
160ml olive oil
3 small red chillies, split and seeds removed
4 garlic cloves, chopped
1 slice stale ciabatta, crusts removed and chopped
50g blanched almonds
50g hazelnuts, roasted
2 large tomatoes, peeled, seeds removed and chopped
15ml white vinegar
Small handful of flat-leaf parsley, chopped
Salt and freshly ground black pepper

Start by roasting the peppers on the braai, turning them with a pair of tongs until peppers are black and blistered. Place peppers in a plastic bag to cool and peel them once cold. Alternatively, throw the peppers on the braai, turning them with tongs until the skins are charred and blistered.

Heat half the olive oil in a small frying pan, add the chilli, garlic, bread and almonds and cook for 2 to 3 minutes. Make sure they don't burn. Cool slightly. Blend the bread mixture with the hazelnuts, tomato and red peppers until well combined. With the motor running, add olive oil in a thin, steady stream until the sauce is smooth. Stir in the vinegar and parsley and season.

To cook the tuna, the braai grid should be well oiled and very clean. Drizzle the tuna steaks with a little olive oil and sprinkle salt on both sides. Place on a medium fire and braai for about 2 minutes until a nice crust has formed. Turn over and braai for a minute more.

Lightly oil the leeks and braai until nicely charred.

Put the tuna steaks on a plate, top with the Romesco sauce and braaied leeks. Drizzle with lemon juice.

Please forgive me for dressing our beloved boerewors in an Eastern sauce.

INGREDIENTS

16 beef chipolatas

125ml Teriyaki sauce
125ml water
30ml English or wholegrain mustard

Place the Teriyaki, water and mustard in a medium saucepan. Cook over high heat for 2 to 3 minutes until thickened. Place it on the cooler side of the braai to keep it warm.

Braai sausages directly on the braai until braaied through. Add to the warm sauce and eat immediately.

OPTIONAL: Serve with some noodles and chopped coriander and spring onions.

HALOUMI WITH POMEGRANATE-MINT SALSA

This pomegranate-mint salsa is quite versatile — it can be used on lamb and chicken dishes as well.

INGREDIENTS

400g haloumi, sliced in 1cm thickness

A handful of mint leaves, chopped
120g pomegranate seeds
30ml chopped spring onion
250ml olive oil
2 garlic cloves, finely chopped
30ml lemon zest
15ml lemon juice
Salt and freshly ground black pepper

Combine the mint leaves, pomegranate seeds, spring onion, olive oil, garlic cloves, lemon zest and juice in a small bowl. Set aside.

Braai the haloumi in an oiled griddle pan over medium-to-high heat, turning once. Remove from the griddle pan and transfer onto a platter. Spoon the pomegranate and mint salsa over the cheese.

T-BONE FLORENTINE

T-bone steak is the main act here. Forget the fancy name, just chop the herbs and get the fire going. I prefer my T-bone rare. Braai it a bit longer for medium.

INGREDIENTS

4 T-bone steaks (2cm thick, 350g in size)

125g unsalted butter, softened to room temperature

4 garlic cloves, chopped

60ml chopped flat-leaf parsley

Salt and freshly ground black pepper

4 lemons, cut in half

Bring the steaks to room temperature an hour before the braai.

Blend the butter with the chopped garlic, parsley and seasoning.

Rub the halved lemons over the steaks and season them with salt and pepper. Braai on a medium-to-high heat for 4 to 5 minutes per side. Braai the lemon halves at the same time.

Remove the T-bones from the fire, top the steaks with the butter and serve with the braaied lemon on the side.

PORK CHOPS
WITH STRAWBERRY AND BALSAMIC VINEGAR SAUCE

Pork does not like heat. Sear chops over the coals then move it a cooler side of the fire.

INGREDIENTS

4 pork chops (about 240g each)
Salt and freshly ground black pepper

250g strawberries
60ml balsamic vinegar
30ml castor sugar
60ml chicken or vegetable stock
Basil leaves to garnish

Halve the strawberries and add them to the vinegar and sugar.

Heat a frying pan over medium-to-low heat and add the stock. Bring it to the boil. Add the strawberry-vinegar mixture to the stock and reduce the heat to low. Heat the strawberries through. Set the sauce aside.

Season the pork chops with salt and black pepper. Braai the pork chops on an oiled grid, medium fire for 6–7 minutes per side.

Place the chops on a platter and pour the strawberry sauce over. Garnish with torn basil.

GREEK FISH SOSATIES WITH TZAZIKI

Chunks of kingklip or any firm white fish can be used for this Greek-inspired recipe. Clean and oil your braai grid very well to make sure that the fish kebabs don't stick, or use a pan.

INGREDIENTS

750g skinless kingklip, cubed

90ml olive oil, plus some for drizzling

Juice and finely grated zest of 2 lemons

45ml dried oregano

1 garlic clove, crushed

30ml red wine vinegar

Baby tomatoes, cut in half (optional)

Pita bread to serve

Wooden skewers soaked for 15 minutes in cold water

TZAZIKI

1 cucumber, grated

1 garlic clove, crushed

250ml Greek yoghurt

45ml chopped mint (optional)

Salt and freshly ground black pepper

Put the fish in a non-metallic dish with rest of the ingredients. Cover and refrigerate.

TZAZIKI

Put the grated cucumber in a clean dish towel and squeeze out all the excess liquid. Put in a bowl with the remaining ingredients, season and combine well. Refrigerate until serving.

Remove the fish from the marinade, drain and pat dry with some kitchen towel. Thread onto the skewers and drizzle with some olive oil. Braai the sosaties on a medium-to-high heat for 2–3 minutes per side or until braai marks appear.

Braai the pita breads both sides for a few seconds until warmed through.

Serve the fish sosaties with the pita bread, tzaziki and baby tomatoes (if using).

Try the peri-peri sauce on chicken or pork chops too.

INGREDIENTS

20 large raw prawns, unpeeled

Lemon wedges

PERI-PERI SAUCE

4 red chillies

8 garlic cloves, unpeeled

30ml tomato paste

Juice of 2 lemons

60ml red wine vinegar

30ml smoked paprika

90ml olive oil

Wooden skewers soaked for 15 minutes in cold water

Place the chillies and garlic in a small frying pan over a medium heat and dry fry for 5 minutes. It should start to blacken. When cool, peel the garlic and deseed the chillies. Blend with the remaining ingredients until smooth to make a sauce. Season with salt.

Remove the heads and legs of the prawns. Using kitchen scissors, cut a slit along the back of each prawn and remove the digestive tract. Put the prawns in a bowl and add half the peri-peri sauce. Toss to coat. Thread the prawns onto the skewers.

Braai prawns on a high heat for about 3 minutes per side. Braai marks should appear and the shells should turn a deep pink colour. Remove prawns from the braai.

Serve with the remaining peri-peri sauce and lemon wedges.

CHICKEN BREASTS
WITH AROMATIC INDIAN SPICES

This recipe is quick and easy. I can eat this every day of the week.

INGREDIENTS

8 boneless, skinless chicken breasts

125ml olive oil
500ml plain Greek yoghurt
Handful of coriander leaves, chopped
Handful of fresh mint leaves
½ onion, chopped
6 garlic cloves, crushed
15ml lemon juice
15ml curry powder
1 x 5cm fresh ginger, chopped

Salt and freshly ground black pepper
Pita breads

Blend half the olive oil and all the remaining ingredients in a food processor to a smooth paste. Reserve 125ml of the marinade. Transfer the chicken breasts to a medium-sized plastic freezer bag and pour the rest of the marinade over. Seal bag and refrigerate for a few hours or overnight.

Bring the yoghurt-marinated chicken to room temperature an hour before you braai. Scrape excess marinade off chicken breasts. Season with salt and black pepper. Braai chicken on an oiled braai grid, medium fire for 4–6 minutes per side.

Braai the pita breads on both sides until warmed through.

Serve chicken with the reserved marinade and pita bread.

CHICKEN PESTO SANDWICH

Summer sandwiches: chicken, tomato, basil pesto. Need I say more?

INGREDIENTS

- 4 boneless, skinless chicken breasts
- Salt and freshly ground black pepper
- 15ml dried basil
- 15ml olive oil
- 4 slices mozzarella or cheddar
- 8 slices of ciabatta
- Mayonnaise
- 8 thick tomato slices
- 60ml basil pesto

Season the chicken breasts with salt and black pepper. Sprinkle the dried basil over and brush with olive oil.

Braai the chicken breasts on a high heat. This should not take longer than 6–8 minutes per side. About 2 minutes before the chicken is ready, place the cheese on top of the chicken to melt. Put the bread slices along the edge of the braai to toast. Transfer the chicken and bread to a cutting board. Spread the bread slices with mayonnaise, tomato and pesto. Top with the chicken breasts and close the sandwich.

BRAZILIAN RUMP
KEBABS WITH SMOKY TOMATO-PEPPER SALSA

Churrasco is the term used in Brazil for a braai.

INGREDIENTS

- 1 kg beef rump steaks
- Salt and pepper to taste
- 3 cloves garlic, crushed
- Juice of 2 lemons
- 30ml red wine vinegar
- 30ml Worcestershire sauce
- 1 small white onion, grated
- 30ml cumin seeds
- 45ml chilli flakes
- 30ml olive oil

- 2 long metal skewers

SMOKY TOMATO-PEPPER SALSA

- 1 small red onion, chopped
- A small handful of coriander leaves, chopped
- 200g cherry tomatoes, chopped
- ½ red pepper, chopped
- 30ml tomato paste or tomato pesto
- 60ml olive oil
- 30ml red wine vinegar
- 15ml smoked paprika
- Pinch of sugar
- Salt and pepper to taste

Combine all the ingredients for the salsa together and season.

Cut the steaks into big chunks and season well with salt and pepper. Transfer the steak to a non-metallic dish, add the remaining ingredients and work them well into the meat with your hands. Cover and refrigerate overnight. Remove from the fridge an hour before you plan to braai.

Remove the meat from the marinade and pat dry with some kitchen towel. Thread the skewers through two of the steaks and repeat with the others. Braai for 3–4 minutes on both sides or to your liking.

Baste the kebabs with remaining marinade and serve with salsa.

COFFEE-RUBBED RIB-EYE STEAK
WITH A BUTTERMILK-GORGONZOLA CHEESE SAUCE

My friend, Sean Kristafor is a coffee connoisseur and enjoy what coffee brings to the table. Just as a braai brings people together, so does the culture of appreciating and enjoying good coffee. This coffee rub is good on any red meat. Just try it.

INGREDIENTS

4 rib eye steaks, 250g each
Olive oil

FOR THE COFFEE RUB

50g finely ground dark roast coffee
80ml chilli powder
80ml smoked paprika
40ml brown sugar
30ml garlic powder
15ml ground cumin
15ml cayenne pepper
Salt and freshly ground black pepper

FOR THE BUTTERMILK CREAM SAUCE

500ml cream
60ml buttermilk
150g Gorgonzola

Mix all the rub ingredients in a bowl. Rub the rib eye steaks in it and set aside.

Heat the cream in a saucepan. Add the buttermilk and cheese and let it melt. Season with salt.

Rub olive oil on the rib eye steaks. Braai on a medium-to-high heat for 5 minutes per side. Transfer to a platter and serve with the hot sauce.

MEXICAN CHICKEN WRAP PARTY

INGREDIENTS

6 skinless, boneless chicken breasts
2 onions, peeled and quartered
1 red pepper, deseeded
1 yellow pepper, deseeded
6 tortilla wraps
250ml sour cream
Guacamole (see page 130)

MEXICAN RUB

15ml brown sugar
15ml cumin
15ml chilli powder
15ml garlic powder
15ml onion powder
15ml smoked paprika

SPICY TOMATO SALSA

4 tomatoes, chopped
1 red onion, chopped fine
1 red chilli, chopped fine
Handful of coriander leaves, chopped
Juice of half a lemon
Salt and freshly ground black pepper

Mix all the ingredients for the rub together. Add to the chicken breasts and give it a good massage.

To make the salsa, combine the tomatoes, onion, chilli and coriander leaves in a bowl. Drizzle the lemon juice over and season with salt and black pepper.

Braai the chicken breasts on a medium-to-high fire for 6–8 minutes per side or until a nice golden colour. Braai the onions and peppers at the same time. You may use a griddle pan for the vegetables. Braai the tortilla wraps. This should take just a few seconds as you only want it hot.

Remove the chicken, vegetables and tortillas from the braai. Let the chicken rest for a few minutes. Slice the chicken. Paint the tortilla wraps with guacamole and sour cream. Serve with the spicy tomato salsa and braaied onions and peppers.

LAMB BURGER WITH GUACAMOLE

INGREDIENTS

45ml chopped onion
30ml flat-leaf parsley, chopped
15ml Dijon mustard
15ml rosemary, finely crushed
1 garlic clove, crushed
750g lamb mince
250g beef mince
Salt and freshly ground black pepper

Sliced red onions
Sliced tomato
Guacamole (see page 130)
Hamburger rolls

In a bowl, mix together the onion, parsley, mustard, rosemary and garlic. Add the lamb and beef mince with a tablespoon or two of ice water to help with the mixing. Divide the meat mixture into 6 portions. Shape each portion into a 2.5cm-thick patty. Season on both sides with salt and freshly ground black pepper. Make a depression in the centre of each patty with your thumb.

Place the patties, indent side up, on a medium to high heat. Braai the patties 5 minutes per side for medium rare and longer for well done. Slice the hamburger rolls in half and heat on the braai.

Serve with sliced red onion, tomatoes and the guacamole.

MY SPICY LAMB CHOPS

INGREDIENTS

12 lamb loin chops
3 cloves garlic, crushed
2 sprigs fresh rosemary
60ml olive oil

Natural yoghurt
Coriander leaves, chopped

FOR THE RUB

15ml brown sugar
15ml salt
15ml freshly ground black pepper
15ml ground cumin
15ml ground coriander
15ml mustard powder

In a small bowl, mix the ingredients for the rub.

Marinate the chops in the garlic, rosemary and olive oil. Add the rub and mix well onto the oiled meat.

Braai the lamb chops on a well-oiled grid at a medium-to-high heat for 5–6 minutes per side for medium rare. Remove from the braai and serve with natural yoghurt and chopped coriander (optional).

LATIN MOJO PORK FILLET

A Mexican-flavoured rub and a marinade of orange juice, herbs and garlic ... can you ask for more? Use the Indirect method for a few minutes if you like, but don't leave the braai. Sear the pork fillet directly on the fire for a few minutes before moving it to the edges with less heat.

INGREDIENTS

2 pork fillets, each 750g to 1kg

Mexican rub (see page 44)

FOR THE ORANGE MOJO

30ml cumin seeds

375ml olive oil

4 chillies, seeded and finely chopped

12 cloves garlic, minced

Salt and freshly ground black pepper

180ml fresh orange juice

Small handful of coriander leaves, finely chopped

Small handful of mint leaves, finely chopped

45ml sherry

To make the mojo, toast the cumin seeds over a medium heat in a pan for about 30 seconds. Add the olive oil. Heat until warm. Add the chillies, garlic and seasoning. Heat for 3–5 minutes to develop the flavours. Remove from the heat. Combine the orange juice, coriander, mint and sherry together and pour into the warm olive oil. Divide the mixture in half and cool.

Rub the pork fillets in the Mexican spice rub. Place the spiced fillets in a plastic freezer bag along with half of the orange mojo. Seal and refrigerate overnight.

Remove the pork an hour before the braai. Discard the marinade and pat the fillets dry with some kitchen towel.

Braai pork fillets on an oiled grid at medium heat, directly on the fire. Sear it for 3–4 minutes per side. Move the pork fillet on its side for 3–4 minutes. Continue to roll and braai in this manner for 15 minutes. The pork fillet will be ready when it's firm to the touch.

Let it rest for 5 minutes before you slice it. Serve with the remaining mojo and some roasted tomatoes.

BOEREWORS COIL
WITH TOMATO SMOOR

We serve this as an item for the children when we cater. Grown-ups love it too.

INGREDIENTS

1kg boerewors

Wooden skewers soaked for 15 minutes in cold water

2 onions, halved

1 red pepper, deseeded and halved

TOMATO SMOOR

45ml olive oil
1 x 410g tin tomatoes
1 large onion, chopped
15ml sugar
Salt and freshly ground black pepper

Coil the sausage into a spiral. Place 2 wooden skewers through the sausage to secure it.

To make the smoor, heat the olive oil in a pan and fry the onions until soft. Add the tomatoes and cook over a low heat for 20 minutes, breaking the tomato with a wooden spoon as it cooks. Add the sugar and seasoning. Take it off the heat.

Braai the boerewors coil over medium-low heat until brown underneath. Turn it over and braai until ready.

Braai the onions and pepper alongside the boerewors coil.

Serve with buttered rolls and the tomato smoor.

GREEK LAMB SOSATIES
WITH CAPER-MINT SALSA

This recipe is for my dear friend, Fiona Mckie. We always end up braaiing some lamb. Fifi, this one is for you.

INGREDIENTS

1.5kg leg of lamb, cubed
Salt and freshly ground black pepper

30ml chilli flakes
4 garlic cloves, chopped
30ml brown sugar
60ml olive oil
15ml oregano leaves
Juice and zest of 1 lemon

Wooden skewers soaked for 15 minutes in cold water

CAPER-MINT SAUCE

Small bunch of flat-leaf parsley
Small bunch of fresh mint
1 anchovy fillet, rinsed
2 garlic cloves, crushed
30ml capers, drained
60ml red wine vinegar
90ml olive oil
Salt and freshly ground black pepper
Pinch of chilli flakes

Season the cubed lamb all over with salt and black pepper. Combine the remaining ingredients in a small bowl then pour over the lamb to marinade. Use your clean hands to massage the meat. Cover and set aside.

Make the caper and mint sauce. Finely chop the parsley, mint, anchovy, garlic and capers. Add the vinegar and olive oil, seasoning and chilli flakes. Set aside.

Thread the lamb pieces through the wooden skewers and braai the sosaties on a medium-to-high heat for 5 minutes per side. Move the kebabs to a cooler side of the fire and braai for 2 more minutes. Cover in foil and let them rest for a few minutes.

Serve with the caper-mint sauce.

Eastern Ostrich Fillet

INGREDIENTS

4 ostrich fillets
45ml olive oil
Salt and freshly ground black pepper

FOR THE MARINADE

250ml Teriyaki sauce
80ml whiskey or brandy
30ml sweet chilli sauce

Combine the marinade ingredients in a saucepan and bring to a simmer. Remove from the heat and cool. Pour the marinade over the ostrich fillets. Let it marinate for an hour. Ostrich is a lean meat so requires little marinating time.

Remove the ostrich from the marinade. Braai on a medium-to-high heat. Turn after 2 minutes and baste with marinade. Braai for a further 2–3 minutes and remove from the fire.

Serve with Chilli Salt Pineapple Skewers (see page 104).

THAI GREEN CHICKEN CURRY IN A WOK

Use a cast-iron wok that fits onto your kettle braai for this recipe as nothing beats the flavour you get out of doing this. A wok will work perfectly well with a bed of coals underneath. How do you know if the wok is hot enough? A few drop of oil will tell you how hot it is — if it spits at you, it's too hot, but a gentle sizzle means it's just right.

INGREDIENTS

- 800g skinless chicken breasts or thighs, cut
- 2 x 400g cans coconut milk
- 60ml green curry paste
- 15ml fresh ginger, chopped
- 15ml brown sugar
- Salt and freshly ground black pepper
- 200g of vegetables such as baby corn, sliced red pepper and carrot
- A handful of coriander leaves, chopped
- Basil leaves

Scrape the thick fatty parts of the coconut milk into the wok. Cook it until it starts to bubble. Add the green curry paste and stir. The true smells of South East Asia will now release. Add the chicken and stir, coating it all in the paste. Add the rest of the coconut milk. Add the ginger, sugar and seasoning. Let the sauce bubble for about 10 minutes. Now add the vegetables and cook for 3–5 minutes more. Garnish with the coriander and basil leaves.

Remove the wok from the braai and let it cool off on a metal table or pour curry into a separate container.

GAME SOSATIES IN A BUTTERMILK, RED WINE & HONEY MARINADE

INGREDIENTS

900g cubed game meat

6 wooden skewers soaked for 15 minutes in cold water

FOR THE MARINADE

250ml buttermilk

125ml red wine

6 bay leaves

A few pieces of orange peel

45ml honey

2 sprigs of fresh rosemary

Freshly ground black pepper

Mix the marinade ingredients in a bowl. Marinate the cubed meat overnight.

Remove the meat from the marinade and skewer 150g of meat onto each sosatie stick. Braai on a medium-to-high heat for 3–4 minutes per side.

SOUTH AFRICAN CURRIED APRICOT CHICKEN KEBABS

INGREDIENTS

500g skinless and boneless chicken breasts, cubed

24 Turkish dried apricots

8 wooden skewers soaked for 15 minutes in cold water

FOR THE MARINADE

45ml white wine vinegar

30ml olive oil

15ml brown sugar

15ml ground cumin

Coriander leaves, chopped

Zest of 1 lemon

30ml curry powder

30ml sweet chilli sauce or chutney

Salt and freshly ground black pepper

Thread the chicken pieces and apricots onto the skewers.

Mix the white wine vinegar, olive oil, sugar, ground cumin, coriander, lemon zest, curry powder, and chilli sauce or chutney together. Marinate the chicken sosaties for at least 3 hours.

Braai on an oiled grid at medium heat for between 8 and 10 minutes. Baste with any left-over marinade in the last 2 minutes.

SIRLOIN STEAK
WITH TABASCO BUTTER

Ask your butcher for a large piece of sirloin. Slice it at home into thick steaks then.

INGREDIENTS

4 sirloin steaks, about 200g each

Lemon wedges to serve

TABASCO BUTTER

125g unsalted butter

15ml green or red Tabasco sauce

1 clove garlic, crushed

30ml flat-leaf parsley, chopped

30ml mint, chopped

30ml coriander leaves, chopped

Place all the ingredients for the butter into a bowl and combine well. Lay a sheet of plastic wrap on a work surface. Spoon the butter mixture down the centre to make a log about 10cm long. Wrap the butter. Refrigerate until needed.

Braai the sirloin on an oiled grid on a medium-to-high heat for 3 minutes per side for medium rare. Transfer to a plate and cover loosely with foil.

Slice the butter into coins and serve on the warm steaks with the lemon wedges on the side.

INDIRECT COOKING

BRAAIED BEEF FILLET WITH CHIMMICHURRI

A real crowd pleaser. Chimmichurri is a flavoursome Argentinian sauce, a mix of garlic, herbs and vinegar, which goes well with just about any braaied meat or seafood.

INGREDIENTS

800g beef fillet

FOR THE CHIMMICHURRI

125ml olive oil

125ml red wine vinegar

45ml onion, minced

30ml fresh flat-leaf parsley, finely chopped

30ml fresh oregano, finely chopped

30ml garlic, minced

5ml red chilli flakes

Salt to taste

Black pepper, freshly ground, to taste

To make the chimmichurri, whisk together the olive oil, vinegar, onion, parsley, oregano, garlic, chilli flakes and seasoning. Blend in a blender if desired or just leave it to stand at room temperature for about 30 minutes to allow the flavours to blend. Whisk again just before serving. The sauce can be made ahead and kept for 2 days.

Prepare your kettle for the Indirect method. Place the beef fillet on direct heat and sear all sides. This will take a few minutes. Move the beef fillet now to the indirect heat on the kettle. Close the lid. Braai for a maximum of 25–30 minutes. The temperature inside the kettle should be 180–190°C.

Remove the beef fillet and let it rest for 10 minutes. Slice the beef fillet against the grain and arrange on a platter. Spoon the Chimmichurri over the cut meat. Serve warm or at room temperature.

STICKY ASIAN PORK NECK

This is my favourite Asian-inspired recipe for pork neck. Place pork neck in a tin foil container.

INGREDIENTS

1.5kg piece of pork neck
2 cloves garlic, sliced thinly
5cm piece of fresh ginger, sliced thinly
30ml salt

FOR THE HOT AND STICKY GLAZE

375ml water
350g brown sugar
4 red chillies, sliced thinly
2 star anise
90ml soy sauce
125ml lemon juice

Combine the water and sugar in a medium saucepan, and bring to the boil. Reduce and simmer, uncovered for 12–15 minutes or until glaze thickens slightly. Remove from heat. Stir in the rest of the ingredients.

Now get the pork neck ready. Using a sharp chef's knife, make 10 small cuts in the pork neck. Press garlic and ginger into the cuts and rub the pork with salt. Brush 80ml glaze over the pork neck.

Braai the pork neck using the Indirect method for 30 minutes. Turn the pork neck and braai for a further 30 minutes covered. Take the lid off and brush the pork with the hot and sticky glaze every 10–15 minutes. Take the pork neck off and cover with foil. Let it rest for 15 minutes before slicing.

PORK BELLY
WITH A QUINCE AND OLD BROWN SHERRY SAUCE

A braai is a serious business for my friend Rene Bosman who always has friends popping in for his famous pork belly and many other interesting fired-up meals.

INGREDIENTS

2kg pork belly with rind
45ml salt

30ml cumin seeds
15ml fennel seeds
15ml smoked paprika
45ml olive oil

FOR THE QUINCE AND SHERRY GLAZE

15ml olive oil
3 garlic cloves, finely chopped
125ml quince jelly or quince preserve
175ml sherry
150g brown sugar
15ml chilli flakes
Salt
125ml water

Combine the cumin seeds, fennel seeds and smoked paprika in a mortar and pestle and grind coarsely. Rub the meat side of the pork belly with the spice mixture. Leave it skin-side up and uncovered in the fridge overnight. Place the meat on a wooden board, skin-side up. Wipe with kitchen paper. Use a chef's knife to score the skin, making sure you don't cut all the way through. Rub the skin with salt.

Drizzle a tin foil container with a little olive oil and place the pork belly in it. The fire needs to be at 190°C. Braai for at least 2 hours, checking every 30 minutes.

Meanwhile make the glaze. Heat the oil in a small sauce pan over low heat. Add the garlic and stir for 2 minutes until light golden. Add the quince jelly or preserve and stir until melted. Add the sherry and simmer for 2 minutes. Reduce. Add the sugar, chilli flakes and a pinch of salt. Add the water and simmer for another 5–8 minutes until sauce is syrupy. Remove from heat.

Brush the pork with a little of the glaze for the last 10 minutes on the braai. Stay close to the fire as it can burn.

Remove the quince-glazed pork belly from the braai. Rest the meat for 15 minutes before cutting it into small squares. Drizzle with more glaze and serve along with some toothpicks.

Get a large plump chicken for this recipe, the kind that you see at a food market. Spray the chicken with vinegar to keep it moist and add fresh herbs such as rosemary, thyme and sage to the beer to help infuse the chicken with extra flavour while on the braai.

INGREDIENTS

15ml sugar
15ml mustard powder
15ml onion powder
15ml smoked paprika
15ml garlic powder
15ml ground coriander
15ml ground cumin
Salt and freshly ground black pepper

1 organic chicken weighing 1.2–1.5kg
15ml olive oil
1 can of your favourite beer
90ml white vinegar in a spray bottle

Mix all the spice ingredients in a bowl to combine.

Remove chicken at least an hour before you plan to braai it. Brush the olive oil evenly over the chicken, then season it inside and out with the spice mixture.

Prepare your braai to a heat of around 190°C.

Set the can with half of the beer on a countertop and slide the whole chicken over the top of the can. The base of the can and the ends of the bird's legs should be even. Place the chicken, keeping the can upright, on the braai; the legs should be touching the braai grid for stability. Close the lid, and cook the chicken for an hour and a bit, but spray the chicken with the vinegar every 15 minutes. Check to see if it is cooked through by piercing the thickest part of the chicken; if the juices run clear, it is ready to take it off the braai.

Transfer the chicken to a cutting board. Take care of the beer can as it will be very hot now. Let the chicken rest upright, still on the can, for 15 minutes. Slide the chicken off the can and cut into pieces.

SPATCHCOCK CHICKEN

Sometimes, I get a request to do a basic braai chicken for children that is just as good for adults. So we use basic kitchen ingredients for this.

INGREDIENTS

1 whole chicken
Olive oil

30ml honey
Juice of 2 lemons
125ml chutney
125ml tomato sauce
15ml soy sauce
Salt and freshly ground black pepper

Mix the honey, lemon juice, chutney, tomato and soy sauce and the seasoning together and set aside.

Put the whole chicken on a wooden chopping board. Cut through the spine. Open the chicken, then bash the breast with the heel of your hand. Rub lightly with olive oil. Brush the chicken with the sauce and keep the rest for basting.

Push 2 skewers through the chicken to ensure it keep its form while on the braai.

Braai chicken using the Indirect method for an hour at a heat of 190°C. Baste with the extra sauce for the last 10 minutes. Let chicken rest for 15 minutes before slicing it.

HARISSA CHICKEN

INGREDIENTS

12 chicken drumsticks
1 handful coriander leaves, chopped
1 handful flat-leaf parsley, chopped
Zest of 1 or 2 lemons

HARISSA RUB

12 dried chillies
3 red chillies, deseeded and chopped
3 garlic cloves, chopped
15ml caraway seeds
60ml olive oil

To make the rub, begin by deseeding the chillies if you want less heat. Put the dried chillies in a heatproof dish and cover with boiling water. Drain after 30 minutes. Add the rest of the ingredients to the dried chillies. Using a pestle and mortar, work it into a rough paste. Add a generous amount of salt and stir and set aside.

Cut a couple of deep incisions into the drumsticks. Put the drumsticks into a non-metallic dish and rub the harissa into them using your hands. Marinate for 2 hours.

Medium heat for cooking chicken drumsticks is best. Place them on the braai and cover. Let them cook gently for 8 minutes, then turn them over and braai for a further 8 minutes. Take the lid off and continue braaiing for 3 minutes on each side; by now the drumsticks should be a golden colour. Take off the heat, cover with foil and allow it to rest for 5 minutes. Add the chopped herbs and lemon rind, toss to coat.

CHILLI CARAMEL CHICKEN THIGHS

This recipe came together once when we were camping in the Helderberg Mountains and we had forgotten all the ingredients for a regular chicken dish. So we had to make a plan. With just a tin of apricot jam, some vinegar and a few red chillies left, Plan B kicked in.

INGREDIENTS

- 100g apricot jam
- 125ml white vinegar
- 1 or 2 red chillies, chopped
- 8 medium-sized chicken thighs
- 45ml olive oil
- Salt and freshly ground black pepper

Combine the jam, vinegar and chillies in a small saucepan and heat until the jam dissolves. This can be done at the very last stage while the chicken thighs are on the braai.

Rub the oil and seasoning into the chicken pieces.

Braai the chicken for 8–10 minutes per side. Check for doneness by cutting the thickest part of the thighs. Take the braaied chicken thighs off the heat and add to the glaze in the pan to coat. Place them back on the braai, turning frequently so the glaze can penetrate into the meat. This should not take more than 2 minutes.

THAI NORWEGIAN SALMON IN FOIL

This is an easy way to braai a whole side of Norwegian salmon. Ask your fishmonger to remove all bones from the salmon.

INGREDIENTS

45ml Thai red curry paste

125ml coconut cream

30ml olive oil

A side of Norwegian salmon, approximate 250–300g

A pinch of brown sugar

Salt and freshly ground black pepper

2 spring onions, chopped

Handful of coriander leaves, chopped

Grated lemon rind of 2 lemons or limes

Mix the red curry paste with the coconut cream. Set aside.

Drizzle a little olive oil on a piece of foil big enough to cover the salmon. Put salmon on foil and smear the curry paste mixture on top. Sprinkle the sugar and season well with pepper and salt. Now wrap the salmon in the foil securely. Braai the salmon using the Indirect method for 10–15 minutes. Remove from the braai and cool slightly before you open the foiled parcel. Garnish with chopped spring onions and coriander leaves, serve with lemon or lime wedges.

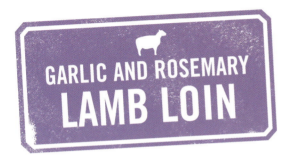

GARLIC AND ROSEMARY LAMB LOIN

I use both the Direct and Indirect method for this recipe. Sear the lamb loin directly over the coals then move it to the middle of the braai using the Indirect method. Ask your butcher to roll the lamb for you.

INGREDIENTS

1kg deboned, rolled lamb loin
5 cloves garlic, halved
10 rosemary sprigs
60ml lemon juice
15ml dried chilli flakes (optional)
15ml olive oil

Place the lamb in a shallow dish. Pierce the lamb in 8–10 places using a chef's knife. Push the garlic, rosemary and chilli flakes (if using) into the cuts. Mix the lemon juice with the olive oil and rub over the lamb.

Braai the lamb directly over the briquettes until browned all over. Now move the lamb to the middle of the braai to cook for 40 minutes or as desired.

CHERMOULA BUTTER FISH

Ask your fish monger to clean and scale the fish. Rinse the inside and outside of the fish under cold running water. Pat dry with paper towel.

INGREDIENTS

1.5kg line fish
3 lemons, sliced
4 spring onions, sliced

CHERMOULA BUTTER

175g softened unsalted butter
30ml coriander leaves, chopped
3 cloves garlic, chopped
30ml ground cumin
15ml paprika
1 red chilli, seeded and chopped
Grated rind of 2 lemons
Salt and freshly ground black pepper

Add the softened butter to a bowl and mix in the rest of the ingredients. Set aside.

Lay the fish in the centre of a square piece of lightly oiled tin foil. Make 3–4 deep cuts into the flesh on one side of the fish. Place some sliced lemons inside the fish. Spread the chermoula butter over the fish and into the cuts. Only butter the one side of the fish. Scatter with more sliced lemon and spring onions. Wrap the fish well.

Put the covered fish in the middle of your grid and braai for 20 minutes covered. Turn fish over and braai for a further 5–10 minutes. Take off the heat, rest for 10 minutes and serve.

BRANDY & COKE PORK RIBS

A favourite drink around the braai in our beloved country is brandy and coke. So let's braai with it.

INGREDIENTS

2 racks pork spare ribs, approximately 1.4kg

MARINADE

250ml brandy
750ml Coca-Cola
300ml tomato sauce
A few good drops of Tabasco
4 cloves garlic, minced
90ml hoisin sauce
Freshly ground black pepper

Combine all the marinade ingredients in a bowl. Place ribs in a non-metallic dish and pour marinade over. Cover and refrigerate overnight.

Remove ribs an hour before the braai. Put on a tin foil tray. Put ribs on the braai and cover the lid. Braai for an hour and 15 minutes, basting every 20 minutes or so. Remove the ribs from the container and put it on the braai grid. Braai for 5 minutes on each side. While ribs are on the braai, pour some marinade into a small pot, bring to the boil and reduce by half. Remove ribs from the braai and pour sauce over.

LEBANESE LEG OF LAMB
WITH POMEGRANATE SALAD

Both lamb and pork can handle sweet spices and go well with this pomegranate salad. I braai this in the heart of summer.

INGREDIENTS

POMEGRANATE SALAD

Seeds of 1 pomegranate
1 small red onion, sliced
A few radishes, sliced
2 garlic cloves, finely chopped
Handful of mint and flat-leaf parsley, chopped
30ml olive oil
A dash of balsamic vinegar
Salt and freshly ground black pepper

1 deboned leg of lamb, 1.2–1.5kg

SPICE PASTE

30ml ground cumin
15ml allspice
30ml ground cinnamon
15ml cayenne pepper
15ml ground coriander
Salt and freshly ground black pepper
30ml olive oil

Mix all the spices together and add the olive oil. Combine. It should have the texture of a spice paste.

Put the lamb on a wooden chopping board and smear the spice blend all over using your hands. Cover and refrigerate for at least 3–4 hours. Remove from the fridge half an hour before the braai.

Have your braai ready at a heat of 200°C. Drizzle more olive oil over lamb if dry. Braai it using the Indirect method for 50–60 minutes. Take it off the braai. Let it rest for 10 minutes before slicing.

Mix all salad ingredients a few minutes before the lamb is ready. Serve the sliced lamb with the Pomegranate Salad on the side.

SIDES FROM THE FIRE

BLT SALAD

I am a huge fan of butter lettuce. Add some braaied bacon, baby tomatoes and thinly sliced onion rings and you have a salad that will keep your guests happy as you tend to the braai.

INGREDIENTS

8 rashers bacon
1 head of butter lettuce
200g baby tomatoes, halved
1 small onion, sliced into rings

BUTTERMILK RANCH DRESSING

90ml buttermilk
45ml mayonnaise
15ml white wine vinegar
1 clove garlic, crushed
15ml chives, chopped
15ml salt

Braai the bacon until crisp. Alternatively use a pan and fry in your kitchen.

Add all the dressing ingredients to a bowl and whisk.

Separate the butter lettuce. Add the bacon, baby tomatoes and onion rings. Drizzle with the buttermilk dressing just before serving.

PAN POTATOES IN THE FIRE

Take the pan to the fire and make some crispy potatoes.

INGREDIENTS

12 or more baby potatoes
90ml olive oil
3 cloves garlic, crushed
Salt and freshly ground black pepper

Boil the potatoes until almost cooked. Slice the baby potatoes or keep them whole. Heat a pan on the braai. Add the olive oil and garlic and sauté, taking care to not burn the garlic. Add the baby potatoes to the garlic oil and sauté to a nice brown colour. Drain the browned potatoes on some kitchen towel and season with salt and pepper.

KOREAN MUSHROOMS
WITH SOY, SESAME & GINGER

This is a recipe straight out of the heart of a Korean living in Cape Town. Thank you!

INGREDIENTS

A mixture of exotic mushrooms such as Shitake, oyster, white button and king oyster, weighing close to 600g

15ml toasted sesame seeds

2 spring onions, thinly sliced at an angle

SOY, SESAME AND GINGER DRESSING

60ml soy sauce

15ml sesame oil

15ml fresh ginger, finely grated

Combine the dressing ingredients in a bowl.

Put mushrooms in an oiled pan and stir fry on a medium-to-high braai fire for a minute. Start adding the marinade while cooking the mushrooms. Take the pan off the braai.

Garnish with the sliced spring onions and toasted sesame seeds.

MELTED BRIE ON A PLANK

It's a good idea to close the lid for a few minutes, but keep your eyes on it and stay close by.

INGREDIENTS

1 brie wedge, about 125g

HONEY-NUT MIXTURE

2 cloves garlic, finely chopped (optional)

60ml runny honey

100g pecans, almonds or nuts of your choice

Warm the honey in a small pan and add garlic (if using). Add the nuts and coat with the honey mixture.

Soak the plank in cold water for 30 minutes. Place the cheese on the centre of the plank and drizzle the honey-nut dressing evenly over the cheese. Bake until it starts to bubble. Take it off the heat and eat with crusty bread.

POTATO WEDGES
WITH HOMEMADE TOMATO RELISH

Potatoes in big wedges on the fire? Easy. Serve them with a homemade tomato relish. Pure bliss!

INGREDIENTS

1kg potatoes, parboiled for 20 minutes
90 ml olive oil
Salt and freshly ground black pepper

TOMATO RELISH
800g ripe tomatoes
15ml fresh ginger, chopped
2 cloves garlic, chopped
180g brown sugar
15ml ground cumin
15ml ground cinnamon
15ml white wine vinegar

Drop the tomatoes into boiling water for 10 seconds. Drain, allow to cool off then remove the skins. Seed the tomatoes and chop the flesh. Combine all the relish ingredients in a saucepan and cook over a low heat for 45 minutes. Puree the mixture and store in the refrigerator.

Cut the potatoes into large wedges. Marinate in olive oil, salt and freshly ground black pepper. Using your longest tongs, braai the potato wedges over a medium, direct heat for 10–15 minutes. Potatoes should be golden and crispy. Serve with the tomato relish.

CHILLI SALT PINEAPPLE SKEWERS

Pineapple on a braai brings out its smoky sweetness. These skewers go with just about anything. We serve them often alongside ostrich, duck and any game braai dishes. Try it with chicken or fish too.

INGREDIENTS

1 pineapple
Olive oil for drizzling

4–6 wooden skewers soaked for 15 minutes in cold water

CHILLI SALT
30ml salt
15ml chilli flakes
A pinch of cayenne pepper
Finely grated zest of 1 lime (optional)

Make the chilli salt by combining all ingredients in a small bowl. Set aside.

Using a serrated knife, cut off the top and bottom of the pineapple. Stand the pineapple on a cutting board and slice off the skin in long strips. Cut out the brown eyes. Quarter the pineapple pieces. Add half of the chilli salt and thread the pieces on the wooden skewers. Drizzle with olive oil.

Place the skewers directly on the braai on a medium to high fire. Braai for 2 minutes per side, in total not more than 8 minutes. The pineapple will get a bit of char.

Transfer to a platter and sprinkle the remaining chilli salt over skewers.

SWEET POTATO SALAD

Caraway seeds give warmth to any dish, although one has to use it sparingly. Add it to one of our country's beloved staple vegetables and you have a good marriage. Use a cast iron pan on the braai for this recipe.

INGREDIENTS

- 1 medium-sized sweet potato, sliced into 1cm rounds
- 30ml olive oil
- 15ml caraway seeds
- Torn mint leaves
- Honey to drizzle

Put the sliced sweet potatoes, olive oil and caraway seeds in a bowl and mix well. Make sure your braai is at a medium heat. Put sliced sweet potatoes on an oiled grid, spread them evenly and cook for 8–10 minutes. Sweet potato should be caramelised and tender.

Transfer to a bowl. Drizzle with honey and garnish with torn mint leaves.

GARLIC & PARMESAN BREAD

Let's make some real garlic butter for this braai favourite. Get the foil out. Have the braai ready.

INGREDIENTS

1 garlic bulb
Olive oil for drizzling
15ml salt
60ml flat-leaf parsley
125g unsalted butter, at room temperature
50g Parmesan, freshly grated
1 sourdough baguette or smaller rolls

Place the garlic bulb in foil, drizzle with olive oil, wrap and place on the side of the braai. Leave it there for 15–20 minutes. Take it off the heat; when cool, peel and chop the garlic. Add the salt, flat-leaf parsley and garlic to the butter and mix well.

Cut deep incisions into the bread, 2–3 cm deep. Now spread the garlic butter evenly into the incisions. Put the bread on some foil. Sprinkle the Parmesan over the bread and drizzle with a little olive oil. Wrap the bread. Put bread on the cooler side of the braai for 8–10 minutes.

ROOSTERKOEK
WITH ROOIBOS & BACON

INGREDIENTS

500g self-raising flour
30ml yeast
15ml salt
15ml olive oil
500ml rooibos tea
250g bacon

Fry the bacon in a pan on the braai until crisp, then chop into small pieces. Set aside.

Combine the self-raising flour, yeast, salt and half the bacon pieces. Add the olive oil and rooibos tea, and knead to make a soft dough. Divide dough into 8 squares and dust each square with some extra flour.

Braai the squares on an oiled grid using direct but low heat. Turn the roosterkoek after a few minutes; make sure you cook the sides too. They should be ready in 15–20 minutes.

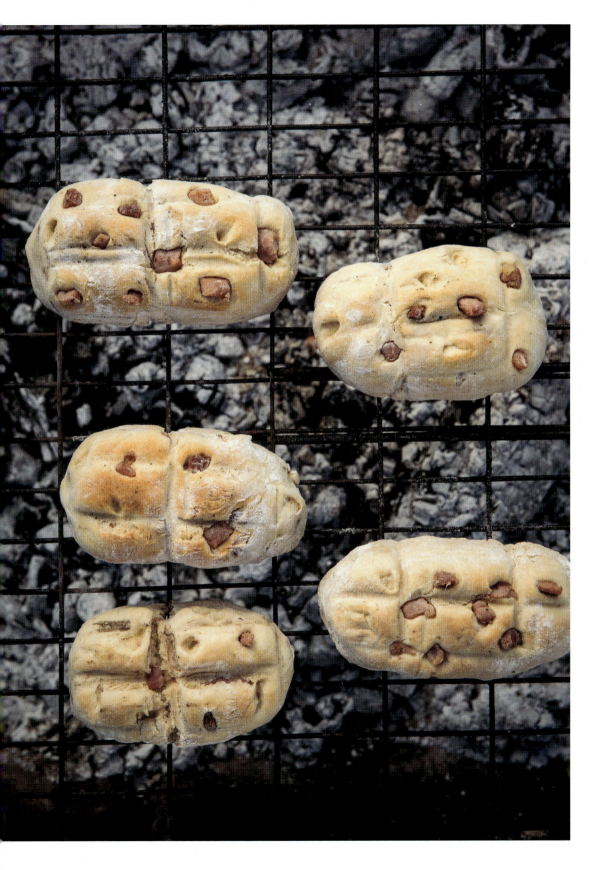

BRAAI-BROODJIES

You can make a killer braaibroodjie with just 2 slices of bread, a dollop of butter and some good quality cheese, or you can make it over the top by adding a wide range of ingredients. When Zola Nene called a few months ago to ask me to demonstrate how to make a braaibroodjie on Expresso, I whipped up a broodjie with bacon, mayonnaise, mustard and gherkins. But that's for special occasions when we celebrate this beloved country.

INGREDIENTS

For each braai broodjie you will need:
2 slices bread of your choice
8g butter
40g grated cheese

Place the bread slices on a work surface. Spread the butter on top, flip the bread around and add the grated cheese to the bread. Close it neatly. Butter the top of the braaibroodjies.

Place the broodjies on a hinged grid with the buttered side facing outward. Braai on a very low heat until cheese has melted.

ALTERNATIVE FILLINGS: jam, onion rings, gherkins, sweet chilli sauce, mustard, biltong, tomato

SIDES FROM THE KITCHEN

GRILLED RED ONION SALAD
WITH FETA & ALMOND-CHILLI SALSA

My friend Coenie du Toit always requests this salad when we braai.

INGREDIENTS

- 4 medium-sized red onions
- 30ml olive oil
- Salt and freshly ground black pepper
- 50g rocket
- Coriander leaves, chopped
- 120g crumbled feta
- 100g flaked almonds, lightly toasted in a pan

SALSA

- 1 red chilli, deseeded and sliced
- 1 garlic clove, crushed
- 60ml red wine vinegar
- 30ml olive oil

Preheat your oven to 180°C.

Peel the onions, remove the tops and tails, and slice them into halves. Place on a baking tray, brush with olive oil and season with salt and pepper. Roast in the oven for 40 minutes, until the onions are cooked and golden brown. Grill them if not browned enough.

Mix all the salsa ingredients in a small bowl, stir, season with salt and pepper and set aside.

To serve, put the rocket and chopped coriander into a large mixing bowl. Add the feta and almonds. Add the onions and drizzle the salsa over the onions.

CHAKALAKA BREAD

INGREDIENTS

4 eggs

1 x 410g tin of chakalaka

500g self-raising flour

90g cheddar, grated

Salt and freshly ground black pepper to taste

1 small onion, sliced in rings and fried in olive oil until soft

Preheat oven to 180°C.

Mix the eggs, chakalaka, self-raising flour and cheese in a bowl. Season with salt and pepper.

Pour into a greased bread tin. Add onion rings on top and bake for 40–45 minutes. Insert a pin or wooden skewer into the bread after 40 minutes to see if it is baked through. Serve with butter and grated cheddar on the side.

ROASTED SPICED CAULIFLOWER SALAD WITH GRAPES

INGREDIENTS

15ml coriander seeds

15ml cumin seeds

8ml yellow mustard seeds

8ml fennel seeds

30ml smoked paprika

8ml cayenne pepper

8ml turmeric

Salt and freshly ground black pepper

125 ml olive oil

1 cauliflower, broken into florets

1 small red onion, thinly sliced

100g toasted almonds

Fresh herbs such as flat-leaf parsley, coriander leaves or mint

Juice of 1 lemon

10 or more grapes, halved

Preheat the oven to 180°C.

Toast the coriander, cumin, mustard and fennel seeds in a dry frying pan over medium heat. Grind to a powder using a pestle and mortar. Transfer to a bowl and add paprika, cayenne pepper, turmeric, seasoning and olive oil.

Add the cauliflower florets to the spice bowl and combine really well with the spice-and-oil mixture. Spread out the florets on a baking tray and bake for 20–25 minutes, or until golden and crispy. Remove from the oven.

Mix together in a bowl the red onion, toasted almonds, fresh herbs, lemon juice and grapes. Add the cauliflower to this mixture and serve.

WATERMELON SALAD

INGREDIENTS

1 small watermelon

250g feta, cubed or crumbed

A handful of basil leaves or mint leaves

125g black olives

1 small red onion, sliced

Juice of 1 lemon

Salt and freshly ground black pepper

90ml olive oil

Cut the watermelon into slick slices, then cut off the rind, and cut the flesh into big cubes. Now sprinkle with the feta, fresh herbs, olives, red onion and lemon juice. Grind over some black pepper and salt and drizzle with olive oil.

BEANS & OLIVE SALAD
WITH BALSAMIC ONIONS

Serve this salad with any braaied meats.

INGREDIENTS

3 red onions, sliced into rings
A pinch of sugar
Salt and freshly ground black pepper
Juice of 1 lemon
90ml olive oil
60ml balsamic vinegar

100g green beans, topped and tailed
1 x 410g tin borlotti beans, drained and rinsed
1 x 410g red kidney beans, drained and rinsed
200g baby tomatoes, halved
100g black olives
3–4 spring onions, chopped
A large handful of fresh basil leaves

Preheat the oven to 180°C. Spread the onion rings in a single layer on a large baking tray. Sprinkle the sugar over the onions and season with salt and pepper. Drizzle the lemon juice, some olive oil and half the balsamic vinegar over. Roast for 20 minutes or until tender.

Meanwhile cook the green beans in a pot of salted boiling water for 2–3 minutes. Drain, then refresh under cold running water. Pat dry with a kitchen towel.

To serve, place the borlotti beans and red kidney beans on a platter. Top with the green beans, tomatoes, black olives, spring onions, balsamic onions and basil leaves.

Drizzle with the remaining olive oil and balsamic vinegar.

CABBAGE SALAD

A quick, Asian-inspired cabbage salad. Serve this with the Pork Neck on page 70.

INGREDIENTS

150g sugar
60ml rice vinegar
30ml lemon juice
30ml coriander, chopped
15ml ginger, chopped
15ml red chilli, chopped
375g cabbage, chopped
1 carrot, peeled and sliced in strips
A few radishes, sliced
1 red pepper, sliced in strips

In a large bowl, whisk together the sugar, vinegar and lemon juice until the sugar dissolves. Add the coriander, ginger and chilli. Whisk to combine.

Add the cabbage, carrot, radish and red pepper to the bowl and toss to coat evenly with the dressing. Let stand at room temperature for about 20 minutes before serving.

CAPRESE SALAD

INGREDIENTS

4 jam tomatoes
15ml brown sugar
Salt and pepper

250g baby tomatoes, halved
1 small red onion, sliced into rings
125g black olives
Basil leaves
250g bocconcini
1 avocado, sliced
45ml olive oil
15ml balsamic vinegar
Salt and freshly ground black pepper

Heat your oven to 100°C.

Halve the tomatoes, sprinkle the brown sugar over, and season with salt and black pepper. Drizzle with olive oil and slow roast in the oven for 4 hours. Remove from the oven and cool.

Halve the baby tomatoes and put into a salad bowl. Add the red onion, black olives, basil leaves, bocconcini and avocado. Drizzle the olive oil and balsamic vinegar over and season with salt and pepper.

GUACAMOLE

This recipe is a staple when I have a Mexican wrap party but also a classic when served with bacon jam and flatbread.

INGREDIENTS

4 ripe avocados
2 ripe tomatoes, chopped
Large handful of fresh coriander leaves, chopped
1 red chilli, chopped
Juice from 1 lemon
Juice from 1 lime
Salt and freshly ground black pepper

Halve and destone the avocados, then scoop the flesh into the bowl. Now add the chopped tomato, coriander, chilli, lemon and lime juice to it. Mix the guacamole with a fork to a chunky consistency.

PICKLED CUCUMBERS

INGREDIENTS

1kg cucumbers, the smaller the better

15ml salt

500ml white wine vinegar

110g castor sugar

15ml ground turmeric

250ml water

1 small onion, thinly sliced

30ml brown mustard seeds

15ml fennel seeds

15ml dill seeds

15ml chilli flakes

6–12 black peppercorns

Start by sterilising the bottles. Give them a good wash in soapy water and rinse them well. Place bottles in a cold oven. Heat the oven to 110°C. Leave the bottles in the oven for about 10 minutes or until completely dry. Remove bottles.

Sterilise the lids by boiling them for 5 minutes. Drain and dry with clean paper towel. Make sure they are completely dry before using.

Slice the cucumber into 1cm rounds. Put into a bowl and sprinkle with the salt, then leave to sit for an hour or two. The salt will draw out any excess liquid. Transfer to a large colander and leave to drain completely.

Put the vinegar, sugar, turmeric and water into a non-reactive saucepan over low heat. Dissolve the sugar, then bring to the boil for 2–3 minutes. Remove from the heat.

Transfer the cucumbers to a large bowl. Add the sliced onions with the mustard, fennel and dill seeds and chilli flakes. Use your hands to mix it. Carefully pack the cucumbers in the sterilised bottles, adding a few peppercorns per bottle. Fill the jars with the hot brine until the cucumbers are completely covered. Slide a butter knife around the inside to release any hidden air pockets. Wipe the rims of the bottles with a clean cloth and seal. Store in a dark place.

PEA & PARMESAN RISOTTO

Pour a glass of your favourite wine and you won't notice the time pass as you cook risotto. By the time you have finished it, the risotto will be ready.

INGREDIENTS

- 1.5l vegetable stock
- 30ml olive oil
- 30g unsalted butter, chopped
- 1 onion, finely chopped
- 2 cloves garlic, crushed
- Salt and freshly ground black pepper
- 300g Arborio rice
- 200ml white wine
- 180g frozen peas
- 90g Parmesan, grated

Heat the stock and keep it at a gentle simmer.

Heat the olive oil and half the butter in a heavy saucepan over medium heat. Cook the onion and garlic in it until soft. Season with salt and freshly ground black pepper. Add the rice and cook for 2 minutes. Stir the rice until well coated in the onion mixture. Add the wine, bring to the boil, simmer, and then stir the rice. Add the hot stock a ladleful at a time, and cook the rice, stirring continuously, adding the next ladleful when the previous one has been absorbed. This should take about 20 minutes. When the rice is just tender, stir in the peas, remaining butter and Parmesan, and take off the heat. Risotto ready!

BILTONG SALAD

Just one request, just one! Please don't use dry biltong for this recipe! Wet biltong is what this is all about. Slice it fresh then add the other ingredients.

Mix the wet biltong with the strawberries, feta, spring onion and red onion (if using). Spread the rocket leaves on a salad plate and place the mixed biltong mixture on to it. Drizzle with olive oil and balsamic syrup. Season with black pepper.

INGREDIENTS

250g wet biltong
250g strawberries, sliced
125g feta, cubed or crumbled
2 spring onions, chopped
1 small red onion, sliced (optional)
Rocket leaves
60ml olive oil
15ml balsamic syrup
Freshly ground black pepper

INGREDIENTS

2 onions, chopped finely
4 garlic cloves, chopped finely
30ml olive oil
45ml tomato paste
30ml mild mustard
30ml Worcestershire sauce
30ml white wine vinegar
120ml vegetable stock
15ml honey

Sauté onion and garlic in olive oil over low heat until softened. Add remaining ingredients and cook over a medium heat for 45 minutes. Stir occasionally. Puree the mixture and store in the refrigerator.

INGREDIENTS

15ml chilli powder
30ml paprika
45ml brown sugar
15ml ground cumin
15ml cayenne pepper
15ml mustard powder
30ml freshly ground black pepper
15ml salt

Use this rub on all red meats!

Combine all the ingredients into a bowl and mix together. Store in an air-tight container until needed.

Thank you Mari-Lise Naude Rabie for this recipe.

INGREDIENTS

1.5kg potatoes, peeled
Salt
Olive oil
Freshly ground black pepper

Put peeled potatoes in a pot with some salted water and bring to the boil. Boil them for 8–10 minutes. Drain in a colander.

Meanwhile heat the oven to 180°C and warm a baking tray inside the oven. Tip the potatoes into the tray and pour enough olive oil over and season with salt and black pepper. Bake for 40–45 minutes. Take potatoes out of the oven and gently squash every potato with the back of a spoon. Put potatoes back in the oven and bake until golden.

QUINOA SALAD

A hearty summer salad with basil and tomato with the nutty flavour of quinoa.

INGREDIENTS

375g quinoa
15ml salt
500ml water
15g unsalted butter
500g chopped leeks
90ml vegetable stock
45ml olive oil
200g baby tomatoes
45ml chopped spring onions
45ml basil leaves, torn
15ml lemon juice
Salt and freshly ground black pepper

Mix quinoa, salt and water in a medium sauce pan. Bring to the boil.

Melt butter in a large non-stick pan over medium heat. Add leeks and sauté until they begin to soften. Add the vegetable stock and simmer for 5 minutes. Add quinoa and oil, stir until heated through. Stir in the tomatoes, spring onion, basil and lemon juice. Season with salt and freshly ground black pepper.

NUTS FOR THE BRAAI

This is bloody delicious. And they go down very well with beer. These almonds can be stored up to 10 days in an airtight container.

INGREDIENTS

30ml salt
15ml smoked paprika
60ml olive oil
500g raw almonds
Handful of chopped rosemary

Preheat the oven to 140°C. Line a baking tray with baking paper.

Combine the salt, smoked paprika and olive oil in a large bowl. Add the almonds and rosemary. Use your hands to mix them together.

Place the almonds on the prepared tray and spread them out evenly. Bake for 35–40 minutes or until the almonds are toasted through. Shake the tray every 10–15 minutes so the nuts toast evenly.

Leave to cool at room temperature. Serve in bowls or jars.

Old-Fashioned Potato Salad

Serve this salad with some pickled cucumbers on page 132.

INGREDIENTS

1.5kg potatoes
200ml mayonnaise
30ml wholegrain mustard
1 red onion, thinly sliced
60ml red wine vinegar
Salt and freshly ground black pepper
30ml chopped chives
4 hard-boiled eggs, peeled and chopped
Pickled cucumbers to garnish
Sliced radish to garnish

Put the potatoes in lightly salted cold water over medium heat and bring to the boil. Simmer for 15–20 minutes or until tender.

Drain the potatoes, peel them and cut into bite-sized pieces. Combine the mayonnaise and mustard and add the potatoes along with the red onion and vinegar. Season to taste with salt and freshly ground black pepper. Toss to combine.

Now add the chopped chives and hard-boiled eggs. Mix the potato salad. Season again with salt and freshly ground black pepper. Garnish with pickled cucumbers and thinly sliced radish.

BEETROOT, WALNUT & FETA SALAD

INGREDIENTS

1kg small to medium beetroot, peeled but left whole

200g feta, crumbled

90g walnuts, lightly crushed with your fingers

Rocket leaves or micro greens to garnish

FOR THE DRESSING

90ml olive oil

90ml balsamic vinegar

30ml honey

Salt and freshly ground black pepper

Place beetroot in a pot of lightly salted water and bring to the boil. Boil for 45 to 60 minutes. Insert a knife into the centre of a beetroot to check if cooked through. Strain beetroot, peel and slice in halves.

Combine the dressing ingredients. Pour dressing over the beetroot.

Mix the rocket or micro greens with the feta and walnuts. Add the marinated beetroot and serve.

A
All Season Rub 138
allspice 90
almonds 20, 100, 120, 144
    flaked 116
anchovy fillets 54
apricot jam 80
apricots, Turkish dried 62
asparagus 12
avocado 128, 130

B
bacon 16, 94, 110
Bacon Jam on Braaied
    Rosemary Flatbreads 16
balsamic syrup 136
basil 30, 38, 58, 120, 124,
    128, 142
    pesto 38
bay leaves 60
beans
    borlotti 124
    green 124
    red kidney 124
Beans & Olive Salad with
    Balsamic Onions 124
beef
    chipolatas 22
    fillet 68
    mince 46
    rib eye steak 42
    ribs 14
    rump steak 40
    sirloin 64
    T-bone steaks 28
beer 74
Beer Can Chicken 74
beetroot 148
Beetroot, Walnut & Feta
    Salad 148
biltong 136
Biltong Salad 136
BLT Salad 94
boerewors 52

Boerewors Coil with Tomato
    Smoor 52
Boerewors in an East-West
    Sauce 22
Braai Sauce 138
Braaibroodjies 112
Braaied Asparagus with
    Sesame Salt 12
Braaied Beef Fillet with
    Chimmichurri 68
Braaied Whole Squid with
    Chilli and Mint 6
brandy 56, 88
Brandy & Coke Pork Ribs 88
Brazilian Rump Kebabs with
    Smoky Tomato-Pepper
    Salsa 40
bread
    ciabatta 20, 38
    crumbs 18
    hamburger rolls 46
    pita 32, 36
    sourdough baguette 108
butter 10, 64, 86, 108, 112,
    134, 142
buttermilk 42, 60, 94

C
cabbage 126
Cabbage Salad 126
capers 54
Caprese Salad 128
caraway seeds 78, 106
carrots 126
cauliflower 120
cayenne pepper 8, 42, 90,
    104, 120, 138
chakalaka 118
Chakalaka Bread 118
Chermoula Butter Fish 86
cheese
    bocconcini 128
    brie 100

    cheddar 38, 112, 118
    feta 8, 116, 122, 136, 148
    gorgonzola 42
    mozzarella 38
    Parmesan 108, 134
chicken
    breast 36, 38, 44, 58, 62
    drumsticks 78
    thighs 80
    whole 74, 76
    wings 2
Chicken Breasts with Aromatic
    Indian Spices 36
Chicken Pesto Sandwich 38
chillies
    dried 78
    dried flakes 4, 14, 16, 40,
        54, 68, 72, 84, 104, 132
    red 6, 20, 34, 44, 50, 70,
        78, 80, 86, 116, 126, 130
    powder 42, 44, 138
Chilli Caramel Chicken
    Thighs 80
Chilli Salt Pineapple Skewers
    104
chives 94, 146
chorizo 4
chutney 62, 76
cinnamon 90, 102
Coca-Cola 88
coconut cream 82
coconut milk 58
coffee 42
Coffee-rubbed Rib-eye
    Steak with a Buttermilk-
    Gorgonzola Cheese Sauce
    42
coriander
    leaves 4, 8, 10, 36, 40, 44,
        48, 50, 58, 62, 64, 78, 82,
        86, 116, 120, 124, 130
    ground 48, 74, 90
    seeds 120

cream 42
Crumbed Brown Mushrooms on the Braai 18
cucumber 32, 132, 146
cumin
    ground 42, 44, 48, 62, 86, 90, 102, 138
    seeds 40, 50, 72
curry, powder 36, 62

D
dill seeds 132

E
Eastern Ostrich Fillet 56
eggs 18, 118, 146

F
fennel seeds 6, 72, 120, 132
fish
    kingklip 32
    line 86
    Norwegian salmon 82

G
game meat 60
Game Sosaties in a Buttermilk, Red Wine & Honey Marinade 60
Garlic & Parmesan Bread 108
Garlic and Rosemary Lamb Loin 84
Garlic powder 74
ginger 10, 14, 36, 58, 70, 98, 102, 126
grapes 120
Greek Fish Sosaties with Tzaziki 32
Greek Lamb Sosaties with Caper-Mint Salsa 54
green curry paste 58
Grilled Red Onion Salad with Feta & Almond-Chilli Salsa 116
Guacamole 130

H
haloumi 24
Haloumi with Pomegranate-Mint Salsa 24
Harissa Chicken 78
hazelnuts 20
hoisin sauce 88
honey 60, 76, 100, 106, 138, 148

J
jam, apricot 2

K
Korean Beef Ribs 14
Korean Mushrooms with Soy, Sesame & Ginger 98

L
lamb
    chops 48
    leg 54, 90
    loin 84
    mince 46
Lamb Burger with Guacamole 46
Latin Mojo Pork Fillet 50
Lebanese Leg of Lamb with Pomegranate Salad 90
leeks 20, 142
lemon
    juice 2, 4, 10, 24, 32, 36, 40, 44, 54, 70, 76, 84, 120, 122, 124, 126, 130, 142
    rind 10, 82, 86
    wedges 34, 64
    whole 6, 8, 20, 28, 86
    zest 4, 18, 24, 32, 54, 62, 78
lettuce, butter 94
lime
    juice 130
    rind 82
    whole 8
    zest 104

M
mayonnaise 8, 38, 94, 146
mealies 8
Mealies with Mayo, Feta & Lime 8
Melted Brie on a Plank 100
Mexican Chicken Wrap Party 44
mint 6, 10, 24, 32, 36, 50, 54, 64, 90, 106, 120, 122
mushrooms
    brown 18
    exotic 98
mussels 10
Mussels with Lemon & Curry Butter 10
mustard
    English 22
    mild 138
    powder 48, 74, 138

seeds 16, 120
seeds, brown 132
wholegrain 22, 146
My Spicy Lamb Chops 48

N
Nuts for the Braai 144

O
Old-fashioned Potato Salad 146
Olive oil-baked Potatoes 140
olives, black 122, 124, 128
onions
    powder 44, 74
    red 40, 44, 46, 90, 116, 120, 122, 124, 128, 136, 146
    white 16, 36, 40, 44, 46, 52, 68, 94, 118, 132, 134, 138
orange
    juice 50
    peel 60
oregano 32, 54, 68
ostrich 56

P
Pan Potatoes in the Fire 96
paprika 86, 138, 144
    smoked 34, 40, 42, 44, 72, 74, 120
parsley, flat-leaf 4, 10, 20, 28, 46, 54, 64, 68, 78, 90, 108, 120
Pea & Parmesan Risotto 134
peas, frozen 134
pecans 100
peppercorns 132
peppers
    red 20, 40, 44, 52, 126
    yellow 44
Pickled Cucumbers 132
pineapple 104
pomegranate seeds 24, 90
pork
    belly with rind 72
    chops 30
    fillet 50
    neck 70
    spare ribs 88
Pork Belly with a Quince and Old Brown Sherry Sauce 72
Pork Chops with Strawberry and Balsamic Vinegar Sauce 30

potatoes 102, 140, 146
  baby 96
Potato Wedges with Homemade Tomato Relish 102
prawns 4, 34
Prawn Peri-peri Skewers 34
Prawns and Chorizo 4

Q
quince jelly 72
quinoa 142
Quinoa Salad 142

R
radishes 90, 126, 146
rice, Arborio 134
Roasted Spiced Cauliflower Salad with Grapes 120
rocket 116, 136, 148
rooibos tea 110
Roosterkoek with Rooibos & Bacon 110
rosemary 16, 18, 46, 48, 60, 84, 144

S
sesame seeds 12, 98
sesame oil 14, 98
sherry 50, 72
Sirloin Steak with Tabasco Butter 64
South African Curried Apricot Chicken Kebabs 62

sour cream 44
soy sauce 2, 14, 70, 76, 98
Spatchcock Chicken 76
spring onions 10, 20, 24, 82, 86, 98, 124, 136, 142
squid 6
star anise 70
Sticky Asian Pork Neck 70
Sticky Chicken Wings 2
stock
  chicken 30
  vegetable 134, 138, 142
strawberries 30, 136
sweet chilli sauce 56, 62
sweet potatoes 106
Sweet Potato Salad 106

T
Tabasco 64, 88
T-bone Florentine 28
Teriyaki sauce 22, 56
Thai Green Chicken Curry in a Wok 58
Thai Norwegian Salmon in Foil 82
Thai red curry paste 82
thyme 18
tomatoes 20, 38, 44, 46, 102, 130
  baby 32, 94, 124, 128, 142
  cherry 40
  jam 128
  paste 40, 138

pesto 40
sauce 2, 14, 76, 88
tinned 52
tortilla wraps 44
tuna 20
Tuna Steak with Romesco Sauce & Braaied Leeks 20
turmeric 10, 120, 132

V
vinegar
  balsamic 16, 30, 90, 124, 128, 148
  red wine 32, 34, 40, 54, 68, 116, 146
  rice 14, 126
  white 20, 74, 80
white wine 62, 94, 102, 132, 138

W
walnuts 148
watermelon 122
Watermelon Salad 122
whiskey 56
wine
  red 60
  white 10, 134
Worcestershire sauce 40, 138

Y
yoghurt
  Greek 32, 36
  plain 48

First published by Jacana Media (Pty) Ltd in 2016

10 Orange Street
Sunnyside
Auckland Park 2092
South Africa
+2711 628 3200
www.jacana.co.za

© Jean Nel, 2016

All rights reserved.

ISBN 978-1-4314-2429-0

Photographs by Myburgh du Plessis
Food styling and recipe development by Jean Nel
Shot on location at Klein Dasvlei, Philladelphi, Western Cape

Weber, the kettle configuration and the kettle silhouette are registered trademarks; all Weber-Stephen Products Co., 200 East Daniels Road, Palatine, Illinois 60067, USA have been used with permission.

Design by Shawn Paikin
Set in Stempel Garamond 10.5/16pt
Printed and bound by ABC Press, Cape Town
Job no. 002812

See a complete list of Jacana titles at www.jacana.co.za